OUR
GRANNIES'
RECIPES

OUR
GRANNIES'
RECIPES

Edited by
Eoin Purcell

MERCIER PRESS
IRISH PUBLISHER – IRISH STORY

MERCIER PRESS
Cork
www.mercierpress.ie

© Mercier Press & Contributors, 2008
First published in hardback by Mercier Press in 2008.
This edition first published in 2010.

ISBN: 978 1 85635 688 6

10 9 8 7 6 5 4 3

A CIP record for this title is available from the British Library

Printed and bound in the EU.

Contents

Snacks & Miscellany

Soups & Starters

Mains & Dinners

Breads, Cakes, Desserts & Biscuits

Guide to Weights & Measures

Imperial	Metric	Wet Cup
1 teaspoon	5ml	1 American
1 tablespoon	15ml	3 teaspoons
	30ml	1 fluid oz
	50ml	2 fluid oz
	75ml	3 fluid oz
	125ml	4 fluid oz

Imperial	Metric	Wet Cup
¼ pint	150ml	½ cup
⅓ pint	200ml	5 fluid oz
⅓ pint	300ml	1 cup
¾ pint	425ml	1½ cups
1 pint	500ml	2 cups

Imperial	Metric	Cups
1 teaspoon	5g	1 teasp
	10g	2 teasps
1oz	25g	5 teasps
2oz	50g	¼ cup
3oz	85g	⅓ cup
4oz	115g	½ cup
5oz	140g	⅔ cup

Imperial	Metric	Cups
6oz	175g	¾ cup
7oz	200g	⅘ cup
8oz	225g	1 cup
10oz	285g	1¼ cups
12oz	350g	1½ cups
14oz	400g	1 ⅔ cups
1lb /16oz	455g	2 cups

Guide to Roasting Meat

Meat	Temperature	Weight	Time
BEEF	When roasting - 150°C/300°F		
Rare	60°C/140°F	20 mins per 455g/1lb	plus **20 mins**
Medium	70°C/160°F	25 mins per 455g/1lb	plus 25 mins
Well	80°C/175°F	25 mins per 455g/1lb	plus 30 mins
PORK	When roasting - 170°C/325°F		
Medium	75°C/170°F	30 mins per 455g/1lb	plus 35 mins
Well	85°C/185°F	35 mins per 455g/1lb	plus 35 mins
LAMB	When Roasting - 170°C/325°F		
Rare	60°C/140°F	20 mins per 455g/1lb	plus 20 mins
Medium	70°C/160°F	25 mins per 455g/1lb	plus 25 mins
Well	80°C/175°F	30 mins per 455g /1lb	plus 30 mins

Why Our Grannies' Recipes?

I like food and I love baking. I also love books. So, as a publisher, some of the most exciting things for me to work on are cookery books. When it was decided that Mercier would publish a book of traditional Irish recipes collected from around the country – the recipes that our grandmothers, mothers, fathers and grandfathers cooked for us when we were young (or even when we were older and just home for some spoiling) – I wanted in.

We thought about how we could compile the list of those favourites – whether it was pies, casseroles, stews, breads, soups, roasts, flans, scones, cakes, biscuits, ice creams or any other recipes. We realised that you use the internet. Thus was born: Ourgranniesrecipes.com

The site helped us gather together the recipes that have been favourites of Irish families for generations. In creating this book of recipes, we have used the recipes submitted to the site by ordinary people: chefs, aunts, uncles, grandchildren and even a few grannies.

For me, that favourite recipe is for the apple tart made for me by my father's mother, Agnes Purcell née Hourigan (after Agnes sadly passed away, her sister, my great-aunt Eileen Hourigan, made it for me too). You'll find that recipe in here along with eighty or so other recipes, sweet and savoury.

I really hope that the book delights you as it has me, and provides a source of culinary inspiration for generations to come.

Eoin Purcell
Site & Book Editor

Snacks
&
Miscellany

Invalid's Bread Pudding

Ingredients

1 tablespoon of breadcrumbs

1 cup of milk

1 teaspoon of butter

1 teaspoon of sugar

1 egg

Method

- Boil the milk and butter together.
- Pour over the breadcrumbs.
- Add the sugar.
- Beat the egg and stir together with the other ingredients (stir slowly).
- Bake in a greased pie tin for 30 minutes at a medium heat.

Jam Sauce

Ingredients

2 tablespoons of raspberry jam

2 dessertspoons of lemon juice

Half a pint of water

Method

- Mix all the ingredients together well.
- Bring to the boil and simmer for 10 minutes.
- Strain and serve around puddings of your choice.

Apple Sauce

Ingredients

3lbs of apples

Juice and peel of 1 lemon

1oz of gelatine

8oz of sugar

Method

- Stew the apples with the lemon for 30 minutes.
- Pass through a sieve.
- Add the gelatine and sugar.
- Pour into a bowl to allow to cool.

Old-fashioned Orange Marmalade

Ingredients

6 Seville oranges

1 lemon

At least 1lb of sugar (or to taste)

Method

- Wash the fruit well in cold water and dry carefully.

- Slice thinly and mash into a pulp, removing the pips.

- Place the pips in a cup of water.

- Weigh the fruit and place in a bowl, allowing 3 pints of water for each pound of fruit pulp.

- Allow both to stand for 24 hours.

- The following day, place the steeped oranges in a pressure cooker (or a large pot).

- Strain the water from the pips and add to the oranges.

- Boil the mix until the fruit is so tender it can be easily pierced.

- Take a fresh measure of the mixture's weight and add 1lb of sugar for every pint of pulp (for a less-sweet preserve, use less sugar).

- Return to the pressure cooker, and boil until the mix jellies easily when cooled on a cold plate.

- Pour into jars and cover.

A note from a marmalade fan

The marmalade really needs to be boiled for at least 90 minutes to preserve properly, and the jars *must* be airtight!

Granny Kay's Stuffed Tomato

Submitted by Kay Redmond

Ingredients

4–6 tomatoes (depending on numbers)

250g of breadcrumbs

1 onion (diced)

1 clove garlic

150g grated cheddar cheese

Method

- Slice the top off the tomatoes and scoop out the insides.
- Mix the tomato pulp in a bowl with the other ingredients.
- Replace the insides of each tomato with the mix.
- Bake in a warm oven (175–190°C or 375°F) for 15–20 minutes.

A note from the cook

My granny used to make these as tea-time treats, and they always went over well. Warm tomato was always delicious.

Granny McKenna's Coleslaw

Ingredients

Half a head of white cabbage

1 large or 2 small carrots

3 tablespoons of mayonnaise

I use Hellmann's Mayonnaise, but you may like to make your own:

1 egg white

The juice of half a lemon

1 teaspoon of Dijon mustard

7fl oz of sunflower oil

Method

Coleslaw

- Core the cabbage and slice thinly or use a food processor to cut into small slices.
- Do the same for the carrot.
- Place the cabbage and carrot in bowl, and mix well.
- Add the mayonnaise and mix very well (add a little more if the mix is too dry).

Mayonnaise

- Place egg yolk, mustard and lemon juice in a bowl, and whisk together until well combined.
- While still whisking, very slowly add the sunflower oil.
- Continue whisking until all the oil has been added and the mixture thickens.
- Add egg white and whisk quickly.

Granny's Northern Irish Stuffing

Submitted by Koraley Northern

Ingredients

White breadcrumbs

Hot mashed potatoes (by volume, use about two-thirds of breadcrumbs to one-third of mashed potatoes)

Butter

Fresh parsley and thyme

Finely chopped onion

Salt and pepper

Method

- Mash the potatoes without milk. Add loads of finely chopped parsley and thyme until the mixture is speckled quite green throughout.

- Add breadcrumbs to the mashed potato, season with salt and pepper to taste, and work in lots of butter with your hands until the texture feels soft.

- This is very light and fluffy when cooked, and even improves after being left overnight in the cooked bird (always cook birds immediately after stuffing; do not let them sit overnight already stuffed).

A note from Koraley

It tastes simply wonderful with chicken or turkey.

Nanny's Simple Potato Cakes

Submitted by Sharon Collins from Meath

Ingredients

Cold, mashed potato, preferably left over
from the day before

Flour (for every teacup of potato, Nanny used about
half a teacup of flour)

Butter for frying

Method

- Mash the spud with the heel of a cup, and keep adding flour until you have a crumbly dough that you can roll out to a thickness of about 1cm.

- Roll into a round and cut into triangles.

- Fry in butter in an iron frying pan. They should go a bit black (that's Okay though – they taste fab).

A note from Sharon

My nanny in County Offaly taught me this recipe, and she would make spud bread for us when we went down to see her for holidays. To serve these, she would split them through the middle with a thread, and put a knob of butter in each one so it melted and was yummy. We had these with the fry on a Sunday in her kitchen. Serve with bacon and eggs and black pudding!

Grand-aunt Nell's Beef Tea

Submitted by Grannymar (Marie Parker)

Ingredients

400g of shin, flank or skirt of beef
(this is enough for two helpings)

500ml of water

½ teaspoon of salt

Method

- Wipe the meat and trim off all visible fat; cut into cubes (2cm).

- Put the meat into an ovenproof casserole or basin, and add the water and salt.

- Cover the container with a lid, and cook in the oven for 3 hours at 140°C/280°F.

- Strain the liquid through a muslin or a fine sieve, and allow to cool.

- Skim any fat from the top.

- Reheat, without boiling, and serve as a light soup or beverage with toast or dry biscuits.

A note from Grannymar (Marie Parker)

Grand-aunt Nell (1894–1997) gave me this recipe about thirty years ago. It was a regular for invalid cookery or nursing mothers.

My Mayo Gran used to call this 'Poor Man's Fare'

Submitted by Anonymous

Ingredients
3–4 pieces of bacon

2 cups of chopped onion

2 mashed potatoes

Method
- Chop and fry 3 or 4 pieces of bacon.
- Add the two cups of chopped onions to the bacon fat.
- Cook until softened.
- Pour a cup of 'top milk' (cream) on top, with a good sprinkle of black pepper.
- Pour over rough mashed potato.

A note from Anonymous
To be accompanied by the remark: 'T'will fill a hole!'

Fish Croquettes

Ingredients

12oz of cold cooked fish

1oz of flour

1oz of butter

1 gill (¼ of a pint) of milk

1 egg

Breadcrumbs

1 sprig of parsley

Method

- Remove all skin and bone from the fish, and flake it finely.
- Make a paste with the milk and flour, and season it nicely.
- Add the fish and paste together.
- Form into croquettes.
- Coat with egg and breadcrumbs.
- Shallow or deep-fry until golden brown.
- Garnish with parsley.

Glazed Sausage Rolls

Ingredients

A batch of pastry

6 uncooked sausages

Method

- Cut the pastry into small squares.

- Cut the sausages in half, and place them on one side of the square.

- Fold the square across over the sausage and seal with a little water.

- Bake in a medium oven until nicely cooked.

- A few minutes before removing, brush the tops with a little beaten egg to give a nice glazed look.

Chicken Croquettes

Ingredients

3oz of cooked chicken

1oz of cooked ham

½oz of butter

¼oz of flour

Half a gill (⅛ of a pint) of stock or milk

Parsley

1 egg

Breadcrumbs

Method

Chop the chicken and ham finely.

- Make a sauce with the butter, flour and stock.
- Put in the chicken and ham, and add some parsley.
- Form into croquettes.
- Coat with egg and breadcrumbs.
- Shallow or deep-fry until golden brown.

Mary's Vegetable Sausage

Ingredients

3 onions

3 carrots

2 parsnips

Half a pint of peas

Parsley, pepper and salt

2 eggs

8oz of breadcrumbs

Method

- Boil the carrots, onions and parsnips; chop them up very small when cooked.
- Cook the peas, and pound them when cooked.
- Mix all the vegetables together.
- Add the parsley, salt and pepper to season (according to taste). Mix thoroughly.
- Roll into pieces about the size of a standard sausage, and dip into the beaten egg and breadcrumbs.
- Fry and serve.

A note from the editor

I was really surprised by this one. Who would have thought vegetarianism was *en vogue* in Ireland in the past?

A Nice Potato Bake

Ingredients

6 large potatoes

250g of cheddar cheese

Method

- Boil and mash the potatoes.
- Line a baking dish with butter; then layer half the mashed potatoes in it.
- Grate the cheese and layer half of it over the bottom layer of mash.
- Build a second layer of mash before layering the last of the cheese on top.
- Bake for about 20 minutes at 140°C.

Granny Murphy's Mushroom Toast

Ingredients

¼lb of mushrooms

½oz of butter

2 eggs

Peppers

Salt

Cayenne pepper

Small rounds of toast

Method

- Melt the butter in a pan, and fry the mushrooms (diced) for 3 minutes.

- Add the eggs and seasoning, stirring over a gentle heat.

- Pile a small piece on each slice of toast.

- Garnish with parsley.

Yorkshire Puddings

Ingredients

6oz of flour

1 pint of milk

A pinch of salt

2 eggs

Dripping

Method

- Mix the flour, milk and salt (gradually).
- Beat the yolk and whites of the egg separately, and add to the mix.
- Pour into a cake tray greased with hot dripping.
- Bake in an oven at 170°C for 25–30 minutes.

Yorkshire Relish

Ingredients

1oz of peppercorns

½oz of cloves

¼oz of cayenne pepper

2oz of salt

8oz of demerara sugar

Water

Method

- Place the ingredients in a pot and cover with water.
- Boil the ingredients for 20 minutes.
- Strain through a sieve and store in a vinegar bottle.

Granny Lily's Scrambled Egg with Parsley

Submitted by Roger Brannigan

Ingredients

1–2 eggs

Pepper and salt to taste

A little milk

A little parsley

Knob of butter

Method

- Heat a pan and melt a small knob of butter in it.
- Mix the eggs with a little milk, parsley, and salt and pepper to taste.
- Pour the mix into the pan and stir well until it is set to your taste.

Lily's notes

Most people overcook scrambled egg, but there is no real concern if they remain a little soft and moist. Whether you like it dry or moist, scrambled egg is never the same without hot buttered toast.

Soups
&
Starters

Parsnip Starter

Ingredients

3 or 4 parsnips

Peppers to season

Enough milk to cover

Knob of butter

Method

- Slice the parsnips and lay in a baking tray.
- Pour enough milk to cover them.
- Season the dish with salt, butter and some sliced peppers.
- Bake until browned and soft.

A Special Lentil Soup

Ingredients

4oz of lentils

1 onion

1 carrot

1 turnip

2 stalks of celery

1oz of butter or dripping

1oz of flour

Half a pint of milk

Salt and pepper to flavour

1½ pints of cold water

Method

- Wash the lentils and add the other vegetables (sliced according to taste) to the water. Boil until the lentils are soft (usually about 90 minutes).

- Sieve the mix and blend in the flour and butter together over the heat.

- Slowly add the milk to the soup, bringing it gradually to the boil.

- Season to taste and serve.

Phil Young's Gran's Potato Soup

Submitted by Phil Young

Ingredients (serves 4)

4 large potatoes

2 onions

3 sticks of celery

2 tablespoons of butter

1 cup of milk

1 cup of chicken broth

Half a teaspoon of paprika

Quarter of a teaspoon of pepper

Method

- Peel and dice the potatoes. Slice the onions and celery.
- Add the potatoes, onions and celery into a heavy pot with enough boiling water to cover the vegetables.
- Add a pinch of salt, cover, and cook until tender.
- Drain and press through a sieve.
- Add the butter and return to the heat.
- Add enough milk and broth to reach desired consistency.
- Add the pepper, paprika and salt (if needed).
- Simmer for 10–15 minutes.

A note from Phil

A cheap and nourishing soup to put hair on your chest on a cold day, as my Gran used to say!

Rachel's Granny's Simple Potato Soup

Ingredients

1lb of potatoes

1 onion

1oz of butter

1 litre of stock or water

Half a pint of milk

Method

- Peel and cut the potato and onion.
- Put them in a saucepan containing melted butter.
- Stir the vegetables on the heat for five minutes without browning before adding the stock/water.
- Bring to the boil and hold there until the vegetables are tender.
- Pass soup through a sieve and back into a saucepan.
- Stir until smooth and then add the milk.
- Season to taste, and serve when nice and hot.

A Lenten Fish Soup

Ingredients
12oz of cold cooked halibut

1 pint of milk

1 slice of onion

1 tablespoon of flour

2½ tablespoons of butter

Half a teaspoon of salt

Some grains of pepper

Method
- Rub the halibut through a sieve to remove the bones and skin.
- Scald the milk with the onion, removing when complete.
- Mix the flour, butter and seasoning with the milk, and add to the fish.
- Cook at a moderate heat for a few minutes and serve immediately.

A note from the editor
When I tried this I was not keen on it, but some people might think differently!

Great-aunt Agnes' Salad

Submitted by Martin Dwyer

Ingredients

1 large chicken

1 head of celery

225g/8oz of grapes (seedless for convenience, red for appearance)

175g/6oz of streaky rashers

Mayonnaise

3 egg yolks

280ml/10oz of sunflower oil

1 tablespoon of lemon juice

Salt and pepper

Method

- Cover the chicken with cold water in a large pot and bring it to a rolling boil. Let it boil for about 10 minutes, and then take it off the heat and let the chicken cool in the water. (This method of cooking keeps the chicken beautifully moist.)

- When cool, drain the chicken of the stock (keep this in the freezer for soup), and then take the chicken off the bone and discard the bones and the skin. Chop this meat up roughly.

- Cut the rashers into little pieces and fry in a hot pan until brown and crispy. Drain well on kitchen paper and add to the chicken.

- Cut the celery into small pieces and add to the chicken.

- Halve the grapes (discard the seeds if not using seedless) and add them in.

- Beat the egg yolks up well with the lemon and seasoning, and dribble in the oil (an electric beater is a great help at this stage). Continue dribbling in the oil until it is gone and the mayonnaise is a 'thick and yellow ointment'.

- Fold this into the chicken mixture. (If you push it into a bowl lined with cling film it can be unmoulded successfully, and makes a great centrepiece for a buffet).

A note from Martin

My great-aunt Agnes was, as they used to say, comfortably well off, as her husband Billy Dwyer was probably Cork's biggest employer at one time. She could well have lived her life without ever going near a kitchen but she loved to cook. When my sisters got married, with the receptions (or breakfasts as we used to call them!) at home in our house in Cork it was Aunt Agnes who came to the rescue and cooked, mixed and carved wondrous buffets for the hundreds of guests. One of her buffet specialities was the above-named salad – this she usually made from boiled turkey rather than chicken, but either works well. I have adapted and adopted it as one of my own, and over the years have produced it for lots of weddings and buffets of all kinds. As she was a grandmother herself (of at least fifty grandchildren), I think she qualifies for inclusion in *Our Grannies' Recipes*.

Nanna's Chicken Soup

Submitted by Heather Osmon

There are no real quantities in this recipe as sometimes you may want to add more or less of an ingredient. I know some people do not like stock cubes, but this is how my Nanna makes it. You can use real stock if you so wish.

Ingredients

1 whole free-range chicken

5 or 6 large carrots

4 chicken stock cubes

Couple of cups of long-grain rice

Couple of cups of frozen sweetcorn

Plenty of black pepper

Method

- Boil a whole free-range chicken in a large pan of water (enough to just cover the chicken) with a lid for around an hour (I use my Le Creuset Casserole, or cauldron, as hubby calls it).

- Take the chicken out and leave on a plate to cool enough to handle.

- Strip all the meat off the bird in fairly big chunks, and return the meat to the pan of water. Discard all skin and bones.

- Coarsely grate about 5 or 6 large carrots and add to the pan (I use my Magimix as it takes seconds and you don't lose any of the carrot juice).

- Add about 4 stock cubes (I use the Knorr chicken stock cubes as I think they have the nicest flavour) and a couple of cups of rice. (Don't add too much rice as it swells, and swells, and swells … well, you get the message. Nanna adds a whole box, but I don't think you need that much.)
- Add a good grinding of black pepper.
- Bring back to the boil and simmer for about 20 minutes (30 minutes if you're using brown rice).
- For some extra sweetness and texture, add a couple of cups of frozen sweetcorn just before the end of cooking.

A word from Heather

You may need to add more boiling water as the rice really swells and drinks up the stock. If you reheat the next day, you'll need to add quite a bit more water and maybe another stock cube or a tablespoon of liquid stock concentrate, as it gets weaker when you add more water.

Caroline's Potato Balls

Submitted by Caroline Walsh

Ingredients

4 cold, boiled potatoes

1 tablespoon of chopped parsley

1 tablespoon of melted butter

200g breadcrumbs

2 eggs

Method

- Mash the potatoes.
- Beat the eggs.
- Beat the mash together thoroughly with the egg and parsley.
- Roll into balls and cover in breadcrumbs.
- Deep-fry or shallow-fry in butter.
- Serve warm with your meal of choice.

Mains
&
Dinners

Jim's Steamed Cod

Submitted by Jim Redmond

Ingredients

3–4 fillets of cod

Salt and pepper to flavour

Lemon juice

Butter

Method

- Butter a plate and lay the washed fillets of cod on it.

- Sprinkle the salt, pepper and lemon juice over the fish.

- Place a saucepan of water on the hob and bring to the boil. When the water is boiling, place the buttered plate over the saucepan and cover with another plate.

- Cook to taste.

A tip from Jim

If you are using a nice fillet, a good way of judging if it's ready is when the flesh comes away from the bone easily.

Granny Jane's Boiled Ham

Ingredients

1 knuckle of pork/ham

Water and vinegar

2 sticks of celery (sliced)

2 white turnips (sliced)

3 onions (sliced)

100–200g of breadcrumbs

Large bundle of savoury herbs (feel free to experiment)

Method

- Let the ham soak in the cold water and vinegar mix for a few hours.

- Once you have let it soak, turn the water to the boil. When boiling, add the vegetables and herbs.

- Simmer gently until the ham is tender. Then remove from the pot, strip the skin and cover in breadcrumbs.

A note from Jane

This was always served with a dainty lace around the knuckle and was a fine delicacy in our house.

Ann's Gently-cooked Beefsteak

Ingredients

Two nice fillet steaks

Dripping

Flour

1½ cups of water

Salt

Method

- Flour the steak on both sides and fry in hot dripping until nicely browned.

- Add the water to the pan and allow to boil for 2–3 minutes.

- Drain the water (be careful to preserve it for use in a gravy).

- Add salt and serve.

A note from Ann

Beefsteak cooked this way will be beautifully tender, and the gravy will be delicious. *(Yes it is. Ed.)*

Nanny Margaret's Pork Cutlets

Ingredients

8 pork cutlets

6 eating apples

Butter

Salt and pepper for seasoning

Method

- Cut the cutlets from the best end of a hock of pork. Trim and season with salt and pepper.

- Melt some butter in a frying pan. Fry the cutlets on both sides until half done.

- Peel and slice the apples.

- Butter an ovenproof dish and lay slices of apple on the bottom.

- Place the half-cooked pork on top of the apple slices and drizzle with melted butter.

- Bake for 30 minutes, making sure the pork is fully cooked.

Nonnie's Chicken with Lemon & Sage

Ingredients

2 tablespoons of flour

1 lemon

2 garlic cloves

4 skinless chicken breast fillets (around 1lb in weight)

3 tablespoons of olive oil

300ml of chicken stock

2 tablespoons of sage

2 egg yolks

Salt and pepper

Method

- Mix together the flour, grated lemon rind and garlic. Lightly coat the chicken pieces.

- Heat the oil in an ovenproof casserole dish. Add the chicken pieces, and cook until lightly browned, turning once or twice.

- Remove the chicken and stir in the remaining flour mix, then stir in the stock, sage and seasoning. Bring to the boil.

- Return the chicken and cover. Bake for 25–30 minutes.

- Mix the egg yolks with lemon juice. Add this mix to the casserole. Return to the heat and stir till sauce thickens. DO NOT BOIL. *(That's how it came written. Ed.)*

A note from Nonnie

This is best served with rice, green veg and a mixed salad. Enjoy!

Aunty May's Normandy Lamb

Submitted by Eoghan

Ingredients

2lbs of shoulder lamb

2 tablespoons of oil

1 finely chopped onion

1 tablespoon of flour

1 chopped clove of garlic

Half a pint of stock (any)

1 chopped dessert apple

2 tablespoons of cream

2 tablespoons of natural yoghurt

Topping

1oz butter

1 clove garlic

2oz breadcrumbs

Method

- Trim the lamb and cut into bite-sized pieces.
- Heat the oil and seal the lamb a little at a time, removing the meat as it browns onto a plate.
- Add a little more oil and cook the onion and garlic.
- Add the flour and cook until the mix becomes sandy.
- Add the stock gradually, stirring all the time. Bring to the boil.

- Return the lamb to the pot and cook slowly for about 2 hours.

- Stir in the apple, cream and yoghurt, and cook for another 20 minutes.

- To prepare the topping, melt the butter in a large pan. Add the garlic and cook for a few minutes. Add the breadcrumbs and cook until just crisp.

- Turn the lamb into a casserole dish and cover with the topping. Brown under a hot grill.

A note from Eoghan

My aunt used to bring this to family gatherings in a huge casserole dish and it was always wolfed down! Great stuff.

An Economical Sheep's Head

Submitted by Rose Mary Logue

Ingredients

1 sheep's head

Bunch of mixed fresh herbs

Boiling salted water

1 medium-sized onion stuck with 3 cloves

Serve with parsley sauce

Garnish

Rolls of bacon

2 or 3 slices of lemon

Method

- Have the head split in two by the butcher. Lift out the brains, and detach the tongue.

- Wash the head and tongue well, and scrape away all mucous material from the nasal passages.

- Steep the head and tongue in cold salted water for 30 minutes, and wash again in fresh cold water.

- Put the head and tongue down to cook in boiling salted water. Bring slowly to the boil. Skim well.

- Add the onion and the washed herbs. Allow to simmer steadily (for about 90 minutes) until the meat slips easily away from the bone.

- Lift out the head and tongue. Remove all the meat from the bones, and divide into neat pieces. Skin the tongue and slice it neatly.

- Arrange the meat and tongue in the centre of a hot dish, and garnish with cooked rolls of bacon and slices of lemon.

A note from Rose Mary

This recipe comes from *All in the Cooking* (book 1), which was the recommended text for home economics in 1961. The recipe gives much disgusted amusement to young people, but may be useful if food prices continue to climb.

Michael's Italian Meatballs

Ingredients

1lb of minced beef

2–3 cups of Parmesan cheese

Half a cup of plain white breadcrumbs

1 teaspoon of oregano

Half a teaspoon of ground black pepper

2 large eggs

1½ teaspoons of salt

Oil for cooking

Method

- Mix the beef, cheese, breadcrumbs, oregano, salt, pepper and eggs together in a bowl.
- Break off into 1-inch balls.
- Cook in half an inch of oil until nicely browned (8 minutes or so).
- Serve with your favourite tomato sauce and pasta.

A note from Michael

My gran used to serve this up, and claimed to have learned the recipe when she was in Italy. I don't know if she ever travelled there, but these meatballs are by far the best I ever tasted.

Traditional Baked Fish

Ingredients

1 fillet or cutlet of white fish

Some quality white breadcrumbs

100ml of milk

Butter

Onion

Parsley

Method

- Place the fillet in a baking tray.
- Cover with breadcrumbs and onion, and drizzle melted butter across the top.
- Pour the milk around the fish.
- Bake for 15–20 minutes in a medium oven (100–150°C).

George's Granny's Cottage Pie

Submitted by George

Ingredients

1lb of cooked and shredded roast beef

1 tablespoon of lard

10oz of diced onions

10oz of diced carrots

2 tablespoons of flour

1 pint of beef stock

1 teaspoon of chopped parsley

1 teaspoon of thyme leaves

Salt and freshly ground pepper

For the mash

1lb of floury potatoes

¼ pint of whole milk

2oz of butter

Salt and pepper

Method

- Heat the lard in a large frying pan. Toss the diced vegetables in the fat and cook for 10 minutes, or until softened but not coloured.

- Remove vegetables and add the meat. Toss over high heat to sear.

- Add the flour to the meat and cook gently for about 2–3 minutes.

- Gradually blend in the stock. Bring to a boil, stirring from time to time.

- Return the vegetables to the pan, and add the parsley and thyme. Season with salt and pepper, cover, and simmer for an hour or until the meat is very tender. Leave to cool.

- For the mashed potatoes, place the washed but not peeled potatoes in a large pan and cover with water.

- Bring to the boil; then tip half the water out. Return to the heat and simmer for around 45–60 minutes, or until soft.

- Heat the milk in a small saucepan, but do not allow to boil.

- Peel the potatoes while still hot and return to the pan. Mash the potatoes, and beat in the milk and butter gradually. Season well.

- Put the meat in a large casserole dish, and cover with the mashed potatoes. Bake in a preheated oven at 180°C for around 30 minutes or until golden and crisp.

A note from George

This is a great winter warmer, which for me brings back many childhood memories of eating at my granny's kitchen table. A wonderful time to look back on. I hope you enjoy this recipe as much as I do.

Ravenscroft Guinness Beef Stew

Submitted by Amanda Ravenscroft

Ingredients

1lb of stewing beef (diced)

3 carrots (peeled and sliced)

1 parsnip (peeled and sliced)

Half a turnip (peeled and sliced)

1 onion (chopped)

Butter (real, not substitute butter)

1 pint of beef stock

1 pint of Guinness

3 or 4 sprigs of thyme

Salt and black pepper

Method

- Dip the beef in seasoned flour.
- Brown in a large pot with about 1 tablespoon of butter.
- Remove and set aside.
- Add chopped onions and sauté for 2–3 minutes.
- Add in all other veggies and sauté another 2–3 minutes.
- Add beef back to pot.
- Add in beef stock and Guinness.
- Add sprigs of thyme.
- Bring to the boil, turn heat down to low and simmer for 90 minutes.
- Season to taste with some salt and a little black pepper.

- Remove thyme sprigs (the leaves will have fallen off and will stay in the stew – perfect!).
- Serve with good old-fashioned mashed potatoes.

A note from Amanda

The chunkier the vegetables, the better! Sometimes, I add some potatoes as a very handy one-pot dinner.

Val O'Connor's Smoked Haddock in White Sauce

Submitted by Val O'Connor

Ingredients

Enough fish for 4 servings

1 litre of full-cream milk

1 small onion (sliced)

1 bay leaf

25g of butter

25g of plain flour

Pepper

Method

- In a saucepan, heat the milk with the onion and bay leaf, add the fish, and bring to a low bubble.

- Turn off the heat, and leave everything in the pan for five minutes with the lid on.

- Carefully strain the liquid from the pan, and keep the fish warm. Discard or keep the onions – it's up to you.

- Rinse out the pan and put it back on the heat. Add the butter, and melt slowly.

- Sprinkle on the flour and stir to combine. This is the base for the white sauce.

- Cook this for a few minutes, stirring constantly.

- Slowly pour on the milk from the fish, and stir vigorously or use a whisk.

- Continue to add all the milk, and keep **stirring over a low** heat. If the sauce seems too thick, just **add extra milk, and** keep stirring.

- Let the sauce bubble for a few minutes to cook.

- Arrange your fish on plates or pile it all into a serving dish with the sauce poured over.

- Add a little freshly chopped parsley for colour.

- Sweet sugar-snap peas or regular peas go great with this.

A note from Val

My mum used to make smoked haddock in white sauce when I was a child. The vivid yellow of the fish made it look like junk food drowned in thick, glossy, pure-white sauce. I loved it with plain boiled potatoes and tons of extra butter. I told my friend what I remembered the recipe to be; her boyfriend, who was doing the cooking, found it frustratingly simple, but the result was, they said, delicious.

Frankie Woulfe's Brown Stew

Submitted by Sarah Woulfe

Ingredients

1½lbs of stewing beef cut into 1½-inch chunks

1 large onion cut into wedges

2 large carrots cut into thick chunks

2 large parsnips cut into thick chunks

Half a turnip cut into thick chunks

2 tablespoons of flour

1½ pints of beef stock

1 tablespoon of butter

A sprig of thyme

A dash of Worcestershire sauce

Salt and pepper

Method

- Gently fry the onion and carrots in some of the butter for a couple of minutes, and transfer to an ovenproof dish.

- Dredge the beef in the flour and brown in the pan a few pieces at a time, and transfer to the ovenproof dish. You may need to add some stock to clean the pan after every few batches as the flour may stick to the bottom, but add the liquid to the ovenproof dish and begin the browning process again with more butter.

- Add the remaining vegetables, thyme, salt, pepper, Worcestershire sauce and stock to the ovenproof dish, put the lid on, and place in the oven at a low to medium heat for 90–120 minutes. The sauce should be thick and the meat tender when done.

- Serve with some floury spuds loaded with real butter and enjoy.

A word from Sarah

This is my grandmother Frankie Woulfe's brown stew recipe. Frankie was born and raised in Ballybunion, County Kerry, and moved to Listowel, where she still lives, in her early twenties. Back in her day, there was no such thing as GM food, additives, preservatives or supermarkets. Make sure everything used when making this recipe is, if not organic, at least local. It'll make the world of difference, and the stew will taste the way it was originally intended.

A Traditional Dublin Coddle

Submitted by Sharon Collins from Meath

Ingredients

5–6 potatoes, peeled and sliced into ½cm slices

1 or 2 thinly sliced onions

8 good-quality sausages

8 bacon rashers

Chopped parsley

Approximately 1 pint of water

Method

- In a heavy-bottomed saucepan, layer the potato, onion sausage and bacon until all the ingredients are used up, finishing with layer of potato and parsley.

- Carefully pour in a pint of water and put the pot on to heat. Never boil a coddle! Heat it slowly and gently, and leave it for a couple of hours so that all the flavours have a chance to infuse and the potato is well cooked through.

A note from Sharon

This is a traditional Dublin dish that my grandmother used to make for Sunday breakfast in the Fifties, Sixties and Seventies, and for dinner in wintertime. It is best served with a heel of batch bread, or if you are a little bit posher than me, you could have soda bread with it – anything to dip in the lovely soup is fine! Serves 4.

Mam's Old-style Macaroni Cheese

Ingredients

1½oz of cornflour

4oz of grated cheese

Half a pint of milk

1oz of butter

Quarter of a teaspoon of salt, pepper and mustard

6oz of cooked macaroni
(boil the macaroni in half a pint of water)

Method

- Mix the cornflour to a smooth cream with a little of the milk.

- Bring the rest of the milk to the boil separately, and then add the cornflour cream.

- Add the butter and then the cheese, and boil for 3 minutes.

- Place the cooked macaroni into the pot and stir in the seasoning (add tomatoes for taste if you wish).

- Pour the whole mix into a buttered pie dish, and bake in a moderate oven for 15 minutes.

Steak with Granny Dwyer's Sauce

Submitted by Martin Dwyer

Ingredients

4 steaks (each 8oz, fillet or sirloin)

Salt and pepper

1 tablespoon of olive oil

6oz of mushrooms

2oz of butter

Squeeze of lemon juice

1oz of flour

8oz of vine tomatoes

8oz of cream (or crème fraîche)

Salt and pepper

Method

Sauce

- Bring a pot of water to the boil, and slip in the tomatoes. As soon as it comes back to the boil, put the pot into a sink and pour in cold water. When they are cool enough to handle, slip off the skins and chop the tomatoes with a large knife into small cubes. Put to one side.

- Rub the mushrooms in a clean tea towel to remove any compost (there is no need to wash cultivated mushrooms), and slice.

- Melt the butter in a large pan and cook the mushrooms until all their liquid has evaporated and they are starting to go brown. Sprinkle over the lemon juice and then the flour, and stir this in. Now put in the chopped tomatoes, and bring to the boil, stirring all the time.

- Add the cream, and bring to the boil again. Continue simmering for a few minutes.

Steaks

- Now put a pan with a heavy base on to heat and, when hot, pour in the olive oil. When this is sizzling, add the steaks and brown them on one side; then turn them over and brown the other side. When cooked for about a minute on each side, the steaks are rare and ready to serve. You may now decrease the heat and continue cooking, turning the steaks from time to time to cook them as much as you want. (Bear in mind that the more you cook a steak, the more moisture it loses and the smaller the steak gets.) Once cooked, place the steaks on a large plate somewhere warm, and reheat the sauce. Once hot, pour in any juices that have gathered on the steak plate.

- Serve with the sauce poured over the steaks.

A note from Martin

After reading in Kieran Murphy's blog 'Ice Cream Ireland' about the search for grannies' recipes by Mercier Press, I was inspired to submit this recipe I had learnt from my mother. While she was alive, this was her ultimate comfort and celebration dish, and as she got it in turn from her mother, it certainly qualifies for the 'granny' label.

The sauce, according to my grandmother, had originally been called monkey-gland sauce because – she claimed – when it was devised in the 1920s, there was a belief that consumption of monkey glands would grant longevity. This particular combination of tomato cream and mushrooms was

73

thought so delicious that it could perform a similar function. This was their story, and both my mother and grandmother stuck to it.

The South Africans, meanwhile, have their own version of monkey-gland sauce that is a fairly revolting combination of every sauce in the cupboard thrown into a pan – a bit like sweet and sour meets barbecue sauce. This is not to be confused with our true granny's sauce.

I put this recipe on the menu in my restaurant in Waterford shortly after we opened, and it was certainly the most popular sauce for steak for the fifteen years we were in business. It was always on the menu as Steak with Granny Dwyer's Sauce.

I know that Mercier is hoping for stuff more in the line of apple pie and bacon and cabbage, but this was a true granny dish, and was enjoyed by her seven children, her thirty grandchildren and (I hope will be) by her (for now) thirty-odd great-grandchildren.

Stuffed Sligo Beefsteak

Submitted by Seán in Sligo

Ingredients
1½lbs of thick-cut beefsteak
Sage-and-onion stuffing

Method
- Layer the beefsteak with the stuffing.
- Roll the steak, and skewer with two wooden skewers.
- Bake for 45 minutes, basting constantly.
- Serve with a thickened gravy.

Haricot Bean Pie

Ingredients

12oz of haricot beans

Salted water

8oz of onions

2 tablespoons of tapioca

1½oz of butter

2 teacups of breadcrumbs

1 tablespoon of parsley

1 egg

Salt and pepper to season

Method

- Cook the beans until tender.

- Meanwhile cut up and steam the onions.

- Soak the tapioca for 30 minutes.

- Separately combine the butter (melted), breadcrumbs and parsley with the beaten egg. Roll this mix into balls.

- Put the onions in the bottom of a greased pie dish, then the beans and tapioca, and a little of the bean water for moisture.

- Lay the breadcrumb balls over the top, cover with a pastry lid and bake for 90 minutes in a hot oven.

A Simple Plaice Recipe

Ingredients
1 fillet of fish

1 gill of milk

Parsley, salt and pepper

Breadcrumbs

Butter

Lemon juice

Method
- Roll the fillet and tie it with string.
- Place the fillet in a jar with a gill of milk and a little salt.
- Leave the jar closed, and place it in a pan of boiling water and simmer for 45 minutes.
- Lift out the fish onto a hot plate and remove the string.
- Thicken the milk with breadcrumbs and a little butter.
- Add the lemon juice and seasoning.
- When the sauce is thickened, pour over the fillet.

Pepper Beef

Ingredients

8–10lbs of middle-cut of beef

4oz of salt

12 peppercorns

12 cloves

1 tablespoon of allspice

1 onion

2 carrots

1 small turnip

Method

- Pound the cloves, peppercorns, allspice and salt together.
- Rub into the beef, rubbing in a fresh amount every day for 3 days.
- To cook, brown under the grill and cut into small stewing pieces.
- Add some Worcestershire sauce and more salt and pepper, and then stew the meat in a small amount of water with the sliced vegetables.

To Cook a Rabbit

Submitted by Pete in Tipperary

Ingredients

1 skinned and trimmed rabbit

Breadcrumbs

Thyme, parsley, pepper and salt to season

Bacon

Method

- Stuff the rabbit with the seasoning and breadcrumbs.
- Place in a baking tin and bake in a hot oven (200–220°C) for 75 minutes.
- When it is nearly ready, cover with bacon.
- When cooked, serve with onion sauce.

Vienna Steak

Ingredients

1lb of lean beef

Salt, pepper, nutmeg for flavour

Chopped shallots

2 eggs

Breadcrumbs

Method

- Chop the meat very finely. Season with the salt, pepper, shallots and nutmeg.

- Mix thoroughly with a well-beaten egg.

- Divide into 6 portions, and with a little flour form into balls. Flatten them to about a height of an inch.

- Cover each with egg and breadcrumbs, and then shallow fry for about 15 minutes.

Cormac's Savoury Sausage

Ingredients

500g of finely minced pork or beef

A little onion

Pepper, salt and herbs to season

1 beaten egg

Method

- Mix all the ingredients together.
- Roll into a single string and secure in a clean, floured cloth tied at both ends.
- Boil in a large pot for 2 hours.
- Serve hot (covered with gravy or tomato sauce).

Mashed Tripe

Ingredients
1 tripe

1 pint of milk

1oz of butter

2 teaspoons of flour

1 onion (diced)

Parsley

Method
- Add the milk, flour and butter to a pot over the heat, and allow to thicken.

- Add the onion and the tripe (cut into strips), and simmer for 45 minutes.

- Serve garnished with parsley.

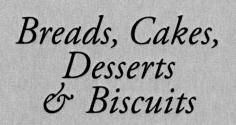

Breads, Cakes, Desserts & Biscuits

Angie's Butter Cookies

Ingredients

1lb of self-raising flour

12oz of brown sugar

12oz of butter

1 egg

Half a teaspoon of cinnamon

A touch of allspice

Method

- Mix the ingredients together thoroughly and shape into cookies.
- Bake in a hot oven (200–220°C), removing as soon as they are golden brown.

A note from Angie

Don't worry if the cookies are soft when they are removed. Place them on a wire rack once they are cool enough, and they will firm up.

Old-fashioned Soda Scones

Ingredients
8oz of plain flour

Half a teaspoon of cream of tartar

Half a teaspoon of salt

Half a teaspoon of soda

Half a pint of buttermilk

Method
- Preheat the oven to 300°C.
- Mix the dry ingredients well together.
- Form into a dough using the buttermilk.
- Knead gently on a floured board before rolling out thinly.
- Cut into small rounds.
- Bake on one side for five minutes; then turn and bake for another five on the other side.

Classic Cream Cakes

Ingredients

10oz fresh butter

8oz flour

Quarter of a pint of cream (which is turning sour)

1 egg

2oz caster sugar

Half a teaspoon of baking powder

Method

- Rub the butter into the sifted flour.

- Put the cream in another bowl and add the well-beaten egg.

- Add the egg and cream to the flour mixture very slowly, beating it all the time until it forms a very smooth thick batter.

- Stir in the castor sugar and baking powder.

- Pour into small tins that have been well buttered and bake in a hot oven.

- Scatter castor sugar over the cakes before serving.

Queen of Cold Puddings

Submitted by Queenie

Ingredients

1 pint of milk

Half a pint of breadcrumbs

Sugar (granulated) to taste

2 egg yolks (well beaten)

Zest of 1 lemon

2 egg whites (well beaten)

Powdered sugar

Strawberry or raspberry jam

Method

- Mix the milk, breadcrumbs, yolks, granulated sugar and lemon zest together.

- Bake at a low heat (100°C) until firm.

- Whip the egg whites and powdered sugar until stiff.

- When the base is cooked, spread the jam across the top.

- Place the stiffened egg-white mix over the pudding and return the cake to the oven at a medium heat until the topping is baked to taste.

A note from Queenie

Some people like this browned, but I love it nicely white and moist. It is really excellent.

Uncle Frank's Lemon Cake

Ingredients
4 eggs yolks

4 egg whites

1 cup of castor sugar

The grated rind and zest of 1 large lemon

2 cups of sifted flour

Method
- Beat the egg yolks and mix in the castor sugar.
- Once this is thoroughly mixed, add the egg whites and beat until it forms a stiff froth.
- Beat in the sifted flour and lemon.
- Pour into a grease-proof-paper-lined cake tin and bake in a hot oven for 30 minutes.

Old-style Rice Custard

Ingredients

1 cup of cooked rice (pearl rice is best)

1 pint of milk

2 tablespoons of sugar

2 egg yolks

2 egg whites

1 teaspoon of vanilla

Method

- Heat the milk.
- Mix the hot milk and rice.
- In a separate bowl, mix the egg yolks and sugar.
- Add the two mixes together, mixing until creamy.
- When the mix cools, add in the beaten egg whites and the vanilla.
- Leave to set, then serve.

Mother's Pudding

Ingredients

12oz of flour

4oz of ground rice

8oz of finely chopped suet

4oz of castor sugar

3oz of raspberry or strawberry jam

1 tablespoon of lemon juice

1 teaspoon of bicarbonate of soda

Some milk to make a paste

Method

- Chop the suet finely and add the other ingredients.
- Mix into a fine paste, using the milk.
- Pour into a mould and steam for about 30 minutes.

Granny Sullivan's Mystery Steam Cake

Ingredients

2 eggs

50g sugar

50g butter

50g marmalade

50g flour

1 teaspoon of baking powder

Method

- Beat the butter to a cream.

- Mix in the other ingredients (add the eggs last).

- When mixed, pour into a well-buttered dish and steam for 90 minutes.

A note from the cook

Granny Sullivan cooked this for years without revealing the recipe. I'm glad she finally did.

Queen Cakes

Ingredients

8oz of castor sugar

8oz of currants

8oz of butter

8oz of plain flour

4 eggs

Method

- Mix the dry ingredients together.
- Add the eggs and mix thoroughly.
- Place a nice amount in paper cases and dust with sugar.
- Bake in a hot oven for about 30 minutes.

Granny Nevin's Batter Pudding

Ingredients

4 eggs

6oz of flour

A pinch of salt

1 pint of milk

Apricot jam to serve

Method

- Beat the eggs together, then gradually add the flour and salt.

- Add the milk and pour the mixture into a butter-lined ovenproof dish.

- Bake for about 45 minutes in a hot oven.

- Serve with apricot jam.

Aunty Margaret's Brown Bread

Ingredients

1lb of coarse brown flour

12oz of white flour

2 flat teaspoons of bread soda

1 teaspoon of salt

1 teaspoon of brown sugar

1 pint of buttermilk

Method

- Mix the dry ingredients.
- Add the milk.
- Shape in a 2lb loaf tin (mix should make at least one).
- Bake at 180°C for 35 minutes.

A note from Margaret

If not fully done, remove from tin, turn, and cook for another 10 minutes.

Old-fashioned Bread Pudding

Submitted by Margaret Mary Mullarkey, from Mayo

Ingredients

Stale white bread

1 cup of currents or raisins

2 medium eggs

Quarter of a pint of fresh milk

A spreading of butter or margarine

Method

- Spread two slices of stale bread with butter and lay across the bottom of the dish.

- Cover with fruit, and repeat the process in layers, making sure to finish with bread rather than fruit.

- Cut the last layer of bread into triangles to give the pudding a neat and tidy look for the table.

- Mix the eggs and the milk thoroughly, and pour over the pudding so that the top layer remains unsoaked. *(When I did this, I left the topmost layer of bread off until this stage. Ed.)*

- Brush the top layer with the egg mix.

- Put on the middle shelf of a hot oven (250–300°C) until the egg mix has set and the bread is lightly browned.

A note from Margaret

Mam and Dad had twelve children, of which only eight are still living. My dad was disabled due to an accident, and couldn't work. I don't know how we managed to survive.

Sometimes Dad had to go back into hospital and the younger children would go visit with Mam. On arriving back home, Mam would make this for us. I don't know the origins of the recipe, but I know if there was nothing else, this bread pudding would always be on the table.

PS: A bit of vanilla doesn't hurt this recipe, though I would avoid the temptation to add cinnamon. Ed.

Stephen's Granny's Buns

Submitted by Stephen O'Mahony

Ingredients

6oz of margarine

6oz of sugar

8oz of flour (plain or self-raising; if plain, use 2 teaspoons of baking powder)

3 eggs

A few drops of vanilla essence or a vanilla pod

Milk to wet

Method

- Mix the ingredients together in a bowl until fully mixed.
- Use small bun cakes.
- Bake at 160°C for 12 minutes.

A note from Stephen

These are especially nice when iced.

Caraway-seed Cake

From Alice McGrath

Ingredients

225g of plain flour

Half a teaspoon of baking powder

175g of butter (real butter, not substitute)

150g of castor sugar

3 eggs

2 tablespoons of caraway seeds

2 tablespoons of milk

Method

- Preheat oven to 190°C/375°F/Gas 5.

- Grease and line a 6–7-inch round, deep cake tin.

- Sift flour and baking powder together onto a plate.

- Cream butter and sugar until soft and fluffy.

- Beat the eggs, and add a little at a time, with a tablespoon of the flour with each addition, beating lightly between each addition.

- Add caraway seeds.

- Stir in remaining flour and the milk. The mixture should be soft, but not runny.

- Place in a tin, and smooth the top if necessary. Bake for 30 minutes, then lower the temperature to moderate (160°C/325°F/Gas 3) for a further 45–60 minutes until the cake is well risen, golden brown and firm.

- Leave in the tin for 10 minutes and then turn onto a wire rack to cool.

Nana Heather's Date Bars

From Joan Mulvany

Ingredients

4oz of margarine or butter

Half a cup of castor sugar

6oz of chopped dates

3 cups of Rice Crispies

Large bar of Cadbury's Milk Chocolate

Method

- Melt the butter and sugar in a saucepan.
- Add Rice Crispies and the chopped dates and pack them well into a swiss-roll tin.
- Melt the chocolate and pour it over the Rice Crispies.
- Cool, and then put into the fridge.
- When cold, cut into slices.

Granny Kate's Broken-biscuit Cake

Submitted by Lily and Hannah McKenna

Ingredients

8oz bar of Cadbury's milk chocolate

8oz bar of Cadbury's dark chocolate

1 tin of condensed milk

2oz of butter or margarine

Large packet of Rich Tea biscuits

Method

- Place the chocolate, butter and condensed milk into a pot, and melt over a low heat. To avoid burning, this could be done in a bowl over boiling water.

- Break the biscuits and add to the mixture.

- Spread mixture onto a tray in a layer approximately an inch to 2-inches thick.

- Cool in the fridge and cut to size.

A note from the editor

By chance, I have sampled this one from the Granny Kate in question, and loved it. My efforts to recreate it were not as successful, but still tasty!

Mrs Neilan's Raisin Bread

Submitted by Helen Dalton

Ingredients

2 mugs of flour

1 mug of raisins

1 teacup of sugar

1 teaspoon of salt

Half a teaspoon of mixed spice

Half a teaspoon of cinnamon

Half a teaspoon of ground cloves

Half a teaspoon of bread soda

1 egg

Method

- Boil a mug of raisins in 1½ mugs of water until the liquid is reduced to 1 mug.

- Pour off the raisin water and leave to cool.

- Put raisins to dry on newspaper (this can be done overnight).

- Roll the dried raisins in flour, and mix with remaining dry ingredients.

- Beat an egg, mix with raisin water and add to the dry ingredients. Mix well.

- Pour into a well-greased and lined tin.

- Bake in a moderately heated oven for about one hour.

A note from Helen

I never actually met Mrs Neilan – as far as I know, she was a neighbour of my granny's. However, this was one of the first things I baked by myself as a child and it still reminds me of my granny: the 'cinnamony' aroma, the taste of the plump juicy raisins, and the moist consistency of this cake that just cries out for a cup of tea to accompany it. For me, this is what baking is all about: memories.

Grannymar's Guinness Cake

Grannymar won the best personal blog at the Irish Blog Awards, so I thought it would be nice to include a second recipe from her. Ed.

Ingredients

8oz of butter

8oz of soft brown sugar

4 eggs

10oz of plain flour

1lb of dried fruit

4oz of mixed peel

4oz of walnuts

2 teaspoons of mixed spice

8–12 tablespoons of Guinness

Method

- Preheat the oven to 160°C.
- Cream the butter and sugar.
- Gradually beat in the eggs.
- Fold in the flour and spice.
- Add the fruit, peel and nuts, and mix well.
- Stir in 4 tablespoons of Guinness and mix to a soft dough.
- Turn into a prepared 7-inch round cake tin and bake for an hour at 160°C; then reduce heat to 150°C and cook for another 90 minutes.
- Cool in the tin.

- Remove from the tin, prick the base of the cake with a skewer, and spoon over the remaining Guinness.
- Keep for a week before cutting.

A word from Grannymar

Guinness cake was a wintertime regular in our house when I was growing up. It was a good standby, and stores for several weeks in an airtight tin. Once cut, it never lasted very long – we saw to that!

Granny B's Jam Slab

Submitted by Catherine and Susan Brodigan

Ingredients

For the pastry

12oz of flour

6oz of butter

1 teaspoon of baking powder

1 egg whisked with 4 tablespoons of water

For the sponge

9oz of flour (sieved)

6oz of margarine or butter

6oz of castor sugar

2 teaspoons of baking powder

5 eggs

And last, but not least, about 8oz of good raspberry jam (homemade if you can get it!)

Method

For the pastry

- Sieve the flour and baking powder into a bowl.
- Rub the butter in with the tips of your fingers until it resembles breadcrumbs.
- Add the whisked egg and water, and mix until a pastry dough is formed. Add more water if necessary.

For the sponge

- Cream the butter and sugar together.

- Add the eggs with a little flour.

- Gently stir in the rest of the flour and baking powder until all is blended together.

Putting the slab together

- Roll out the pastry and line the tin with it.

- Spread a thick layer of raspberry jam on the pastry.

- Spoon the sponge mixture on top and spread out evenly until the jam is covered completely (optional extra: sprinkle chopped almonds on top of the sponge mixture).

- Bake for 25–30 minutes or until golden brown.

- Serve (with a glass of cold milk or a big mug of tea) as soon as it's cool enough for you not to burn your tongue with the jam.

A note from Catherine and Susan

A Saturday 'elevenses' staple, fresh out of the oven, at our granny's for as long as we can remember. She is sadly missed.

Mag's Raspberry Dessert

Submitted by Keelin Dempsey

Ingredients

500g of raspberries (you can cheat and use frozen)

1½ pints of natural yoghurt

1½ pints of cream

Brown sugar

Icing sugar

Method

- Place the raspberries in a deep dish, and sprinkle the icing sugar across them.

- Leave them for an hour or so, and then drain off some of the juice.

- Whip the cream up very thickly.

- Mix the cream and the yoghurt and spread it across the raspberries.

- Sprinkle the cream with brown sugar, and put into the fridge for an hour or two before serving.

A note from Keelin

This works so nicely because the flavours of sweet and tart combine so well.

Eileen's Rolled-oat Biscuits

Ingredients
8oz of chocolate

8oz of margarine

8oz of porridge oats

8oz of castor sugar

8oz of self-raising flour

2 eggs

1 teaspoon of vanilla essence

Method
- Beat the margarine and sugar together.
- Add the eggs and vanilla.
- Add the dry ingredients and mix well.
- Roll into small balls and place on a greased tray.
- Bake at 180°C for 10–12 minutes.
- Remove from the tray and cool on a wire rack.

A Nice Ginger Cake

Submitted by Lucy in Carlow

Ingredients

Half a teacup of treacle

2 tablespoons of brown sugar

4oz of margarine

12oz of self-raising flour

Chopped jellied ginger

Chopped peel

2 teaspoons of ground ginger

1 egg

Method

- Melt (but do not boil) the treacle and sugar together in a pan.
- Add the other ingredients, leaving the egg till last.
- Mix well and place in a buttered cake tin.
- Bake for 90 minutes in a medium oven.

A note from Lucy

Great with a cup of tea. My gran used to slice this and serve it with lashings of butter!

Sponge Pudding

Ingredients

1 egg

1 teacup of flour

1 teaspoon of baking powder

2oz of castor sugar

2oz of margarine

2 teacups of milk

A pinch salt

Method

- Cream the butter and sugar together; then add the egg and beat well.

- Mix the flour, baking powder and salt separately, and then gently fold these into the egg mix.

- Finally, stir in the milk.

- Put into a well-greased pudding mould and bake in a hot oven for 15 minutes.

My Sister Sarah's Madeira Cake

Submitted by Anonymous

Ingredients

3oz of flour

2oz of butter

2oz of castor sugar

Half a teaspoon of baking powder

1 egg

Vanilla essence

Some mixed peel

Method

- Cream the sugar and butter together in a bowl.

- Beat the egg separately and add gradually with the flour, stirring continuously.

- Add the baking powder and vanilla before pouring into a buttered cake tin.

- Brush the top of the cake with a little water and sugar, and sprinkle over the peel.

- Bake in a moderate oven for 15–20 minutes, being careful not to burn it.

Banana Whip

Ingredients

6 ripe bananas

1 gill of water

2oz of castor sugar

Rind and juice of a lemon

1 egg white

1 gill of cream

Method

- Mash the bananas and place in a saucepan with the water, lemon and sugar. Cook gently for about 10 minutes.

- Add the egg white (whipped stiffly), and cook for another 5 minutes.

- Allow to cool and remove the lemon rind.

- Whisk in the cream (again, stiffly whipped).

- Keep on ice until required.

Agnes Hourigan's Apple Tart

Ingredients

For the pastry

220g of plain flour (sieved)

100g of butter
(or another fat of you prefer – but butter is traditional)

A pinch of salt

A few tablespoons of cold water

For the filling

500g of cooking apples
(I like Irish Bramleys, but the choice is yours)

50g of sugar
(free to add more or – if you like a tart tart – less)

Other options include cinnamon and raisins, which I
skipped because I wanted to keep it traditional.

Method

- Sieve the flour into a bowl (the general idea is to get as much air in as possible) with your pinch of salt.

- Cut the butter into the flour (make sure the flour is at room temperature).

- Rub the flour and butter together (try not to heat the mixture up too much).

- When they are mixed, add the water (in stages so as not to over-water).

- Combine the mix using as little of your hands as possible. The pastry should come out of the bowl fairly cleanly.

- I tend to leave the pastry in the fridge for a while (30–60 minutes).

Rolling the pastry and preparing the apples

- Once the pastry has had some time to cool, remove it from the fridge, split it into two roughly equal parts, place it on a flat, cool, floured surface, and roll it out using a floured rolling pin.

- Lightly grease the base of the tart tin, and place the rolled-out pastry over it. (I let mine drape over the edge the second time – a wise move.)

- Peel (optional), core and cut your apples, and place them as thickly or as thinly in your base as you wish. Cover with sugar.

- Taking the second rolled section, cover the tart and ensure that the edges are sealed. (I pierced a few holes in the top, and pressed the edges together with a fork for that real old-fashioned look!)

- Baste the top of the tart with an egg or milk mix if you like to get that lovely brown look, but this is optional.

- Place in a preheated oven at 150°C for about 90 minutes.

Niamh Byrne's Lemon Cheesecake

Ingredients
1 lemon

8oz of sugar

2 eggs

2oz of butter

Pastry (for the base)

Method
- Butter an ovenproof pie dish, form a base with the pastry, and leave aside.

- Grate the rind of the lemon into a pan.

- Add the eggs (whipped), sugar and lemon juice.

- Simmer until the sauce becomes as thick as honey; then pour the mix into the pastry base.

- Bake in a hot oven for 15 minutes.

Granny Reilly's Swiss Roll

Submitted by Gavin Reilly

Ingredients

2oz of plain flour

3 eggs

3oz of castor sugar

2 tablespoons of raspberry jam

1 tablespoon of hot water

Quarter of a teaspoon of vanilla essence

½oz of paisley flour

Method

- Butter and paper a square, flat baking tray.
- Mix the two flours, and whisk the egg whites into a stiff froth.
- Add the yolks to the whites one by one and beat well.
- Beat in the sugar till it is dissolved before adding the flour.
- Spoon in the hot water and the flavouring, then pour into the prepared tin and bake in a hot oven for 15 minutes.
- Turn out onto sugared paper, spread with jam and roll up.

A note from Gavin

Although the recipe doesn't call for it, heating the jam makes this process a lot easier.

Thomas' Vanilla Slices

Submitted by Thomas

Ingredients

50g of butter

50g of sugar

50g of ground rice

1 teaspoon of baking powder

Filling

1 gill of milk

2 tablespoons of cornflour

1 egg

2oz sugar

Vanilla essence

Icing sugar

Method

- Cream the butter and sugar together.
- Add the eggs gradually; then stir in the flour.
- Add the ground rice with the baking powder mixed in.
- Bake in a shallow, round tin in a hot oven.

Filling

- Boil the milk and stir in the cornflour. Take off the heat.
- Mix this gradually with a beaten egg and add the sugar.
- Return to the heat and stir until it thickens.
- Let the mix cool; then add the vanilla.
- Combine by spreading between layers of the cake.
- Sift icing sugar across the top of the slice.

Summer Strawberry Cream

Ingredients
Half a pint of thick cream

8oz of ripe strawberries

Lemon juice

Method
- Press the strawberries through a sieve and whisk in the cream and lemon juice.
- As the froth rises from the mix, catch it on a sieve, adding a little more lemon juice if no more froth is forming.
- Pour the cream into glasses and serve with the froth on top.

A note from Thomas
A great summer treat that my granny served when I was a kid in north Dublin.

Granny Lily's Fruit Salad

Ingredients

½oz sugar

2fl oz water

Various fruits to taste

½oz of almonds

2 tablespoons of raspberry vinegar

Whipped cream to serve

Method

- Boil the sugar and water to form a syrup.
- Slice the fruit into a bowl and pour the syrup over it.
- Stir in the raspberry vinegar and sprinkle the almonds over the top.
- When cool, spoon the cream over the top.

A Simple Traditional Pancake Recipe

Submitted by Blathnaid Healy

Ingredients

4oz of flour

Half a pint of full-fat milk

1 medium egg (free range)

A pinch of salt

Method

- Thoroughly mix the ingredients together (using a whisk to ensure there are no lumps).

- Pour from the bowl into a jug, and allow to stand for a few hours.

- Cook in a shallow frying pan over a low-to-medium heat for 3–4 minutes a side depending on taste.

Drop Biscuits

Submitted by John Doyle, Belfast

Ingredients
2 cups of sifted flour

2 teaspoons of baking powder

1½ cups of milk

Pinch of salt

Method
- Beat all the ingredients together quickly.
- Drop spoonfuls of the mixture into a buttered pan from a height, leaving room for the biscuits to spread.
- Bake in a hot oven for about 5 minutes (more if required).
- Serve hot and buttered.

A note from John
Great with Golden Syrup and tea on a winter's evening.

Eve's Pudding

Submitted by Carmel Hatchell, Cork

Ingredients

4oz of margarine

4oz of castor sugar

6oz of flour

2 eggs

2oz of granulated sugar

3 medium-sized cooking apples

Half a teaspoon of baking powder

Method

- Beat the margarine and castor sugar until soft and fluffy.
- Add slightly beaten eggs slowly.
- Add sieved flour (with the baking powder added to the flour).
- Have the apples peeled, cored and sliced. Stew with granulated sugar until half cooked.
- Put into a greased pie dish, and allow to cool.
- Put the margarine and sugar mixture on top when the apples are cold.
- Bake in a moderate oven for 40–45 minutes.
- Sprinkle some castor sugar on top and serve with custard or fresh cream.

Margaret Healy's 'Fatless' Sponge Cake

Submitted by Blathnaid Healy with plenty of help from Margaret Maguire and Ann Healy's notes

Ingredients

3 large eggs

4oz of self-raising flour

4oz of castor sugar

1 tablespoon of hot water

Pinch of salt

Grease-proof paper

Butter or margarine for greasing tins

Icing sugar

Method

- Preheat oven to 200°C.

- Melt the butter/margarine and brush the base of two 7-inch tins well. Line with grease-proof paper and brush over. Also, grease the sides.

- Put the sugar into a bowl and crack the three eggs in. Place over a bowl or pot of hot, but not boiling, water. Beat with an electric hand beater at a fairly high setting. Move the hand beater around in the bowl to incorporate as much air as possible. Beat until the mixture trebles in volume. This could take around five minutes. To check if the mixture is at the right constituency, hold the beaters up and let the mixture fall back into the bowl – if it is stiff enough to hold its shape for a few seconds, it's ready.

- Take the bowl with the mixture off the hot water.

- Sieve the self-raising flour and pinch of salt into the mixture, and fold in with a metal spoon. Add the tablespoon of hot water, and fold in again with a metal spoon.

- Pour the mixture into the two 7-inch metal tins, distributing it evenly. Place both tins on the same shelf in the middle of the oven.

- Bake for 12–15 minutes.

- To check if cooked, poke through with a skewer, and if it comes out clean, remove the cakes from the oven. Cool on wire racks without removing from the tins.

- When cooled, remove from the tins and carefully remove the grease-proof paper (this is why greasing the tins well is so important).

- Sandwich together with jam. (Add some whipped cream for a non-fatless, special occasion!) Dust with sieved icing sugar to finish.

Granny's tip

Get all your ingredients and equipment ready before you start, as you need to move quickly with this recipe to get the best result.

Chocolate Éclairs

Submitted by Carmel Hatchell, Cork

Ingredients

Half a pint of water

4oz of sifted flour to which a pinch salt is added

3oz of butter

3 eggs

Whipped cream for filling

Chocolate icing or melted chocolate for the top of the éclairs

Method

- Boil the butter and water together.
- Throw in all the flour.
- Remove from the heat, and beat until mixture is very smooth and until it leaves the side of the saucepan. Allow to cool.
- Add the eggs.
- Put the mixture into a large piping bag, and pipe onto a baking tray; alternatively, spoon the mixture into éclair tins.
- Bake in a hot oven until firm and well dried out in the centre (about 30 minutes).
- Cool on a wire tray.
- Fill centres with whipped sweetened cream.
- Ice the tops with chocolate.

Apple Brack

Submitted by Carmel Hatchell, Cork

Ingredients

1lb of cooking apples

8oz of margarine

½lb of brown sugar

2 teaspoons of mixed spice

2 large eggs

8oz of raisins

½lb sultanas

4oz of cherries (if liked)

4oz of chopped walnuts

1 teaspoon of baking powder

12oz of plain flour (or 6oz of plain white and 6oz of wholemeal flour)

Method

- Stew the apples with sugar and water until soft.
- Add the margarine and stir until melted. Leave aside until cold.
- Stir in the baking powder, beaten eggs and sieved flour and spice. Stir in the rest of the ingredients.
- Line tins with greased grease-proof or baking paper.
- Divide mixture between two loaf tins, and bake in a preheated oven (150°C) for 90–120 minutes.

Brown Fruit Loaf

Submitted by Mary Donnellan – who usually uses fistfuls but went to a lot of trouble to weigh everything for the book!

Ingredients

20ozs of white flour

1 teaspoon of mixed spice

4ozs of brown sugar

4ozs of margarine or butter

1 teaspoon of bread soda

1lb fruit of choice (raisins, sultanas, etc.)

2 tablespoons of dark treacle (heated)

2 eggs

½ bottle of stout

½ pint of buttermilk

Method

- Mix the dry ingredients and fruit.
- Rub in the margarine or butter.
- Add the slightly beaten eggs, treacle and buttermilk, and mix well.
- Put into a greased 10-inch tin and bake for one hour at 180°C.

Brown Soda Bread

Submitted by Mary Donnellan

Ingredients

20ozs of white flour

4ozs of bread bran

2ozs of margarine or butter

1 teaspoon of bread soda

¾ pint of buttermilk

Method

- Mix the dry ingredients.
- Rub in the margarine or butter.
- Add in the buttermilk. Knead lightly.
- Bake on a floured baking sheet for 30–35 minutes at 180°C.

Index

Notes

Notes

Notes

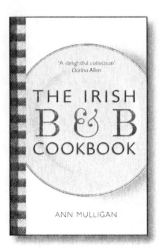

The Irish B&B Cookbook
Ann Mulligan
Foreword by Darina Allen
ISBN: 978 1 85635 583 4

Containing a selection of recipes
which will delight both beginners and
accomplished cooks, *The Irish B&B
Cookbook* is a great find for anyone
who wants to entertain with confidence.

Praise for Ann Mulligan's B&B 'An Bohreen':
'... an irresistible mix of great cooking ...
a B&B which really over-delivers on every
front.'   – *Bridgestone Guide*

MERCIER PRESS
IRISH PUBLISHER – IRISH STORY

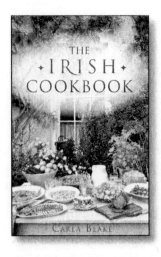

The Irish Cookbook
Carla Blake
Foreword by Myrtle Allen
ISBN: 978 1 85635 504 9

Traditional and modern Irish recipes
sit side by side in this fully updated
edition of the best-selling *Irish
Cookbook*, bringing out the real
flavour of Ireland.

'The first book you need and a book you
will always need.' – Myrtle Allen

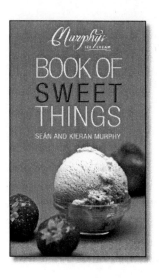

Murphys Ice Cream
Book of Sweet Things
Seán & Kieran Murphy
ISBN: 978 1 85635 584 1

These award-winning recipes come to you straight from the Murphys Ice Cream kitchen, guiding you through the process of making sumptuous ice cream and other utterly delicious sweet things at home.

'Chocolate, vanilla, charm, passion, energy, wit and good humour. The Murphy Brothers ... have great taste and they have it in buckets.' – Patsey Murphy, *The Irish Times Magazine*

MERCIER PRESS
IRISH PUBLISHER – IRISH STORY

Like Mam Used to Bake
Rosanne Hewitt-Cromwell
ISBN: 978 1 78117 156 1

Rosanne Hewitt-Cromwell has been locked in a love affair with cakes and baking for as long as she can remember. *Like Mam Used to Bake* includes favourites from Rosanne's popular baking blog, alongside a whole host of delicious new recipes based on childhood memories and experiments in her kitchen.